To Parents

The Ladybird *First Picture Dictionary* introduces children to letter shapes, letter sounds and alphabetical order – vital first steps in learning to read.

Here are some suggestions to help your child make the fullest use of this book:

* The sound and word game How many words can your child think of beginning, say, with the sound p... Turn to the letter p and see how many of these words are in the dictionary.

* Test your memory Choose a letter of the alphabet and spend several minutes looking at the words and pictures. Cover the pages. How many words can you and your child remember?

* Find the word Open the book and choose a word. Then close the book and ask your child to find it again. See if he or she can find it before you count to ten!

Ladybird books are widely available, but in case of difficulty may be ordered by post or telephone from:

Ladybird Books – Cash Sales Department
Littlegate Road Paignton Devon TQ3 3BE
Telephone 0803 554761

A catalogue record for this book is available from the British Library

Published by Ladybird Books Ltd Loughborough Leicestershire UK
Ladybird Books Inc Auburn Maine 04210 USA

First
Picture
Dictionary

illustrated by GAYNOR BERRY

Ladybird

Aa

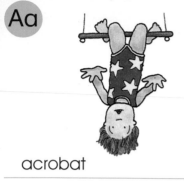

acrobat

anchor

aeroplane

apple

alligator

astronaut

Bb

ball

bird

banana

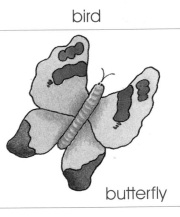

butterfly

basket

buttons

Cc

car

chair

castle

clock

cat

clown

Dd

digger

doll

dinosaur

drum

dog

duck

Ee

eagle

elephant

earrings

envelope

egg

explorer

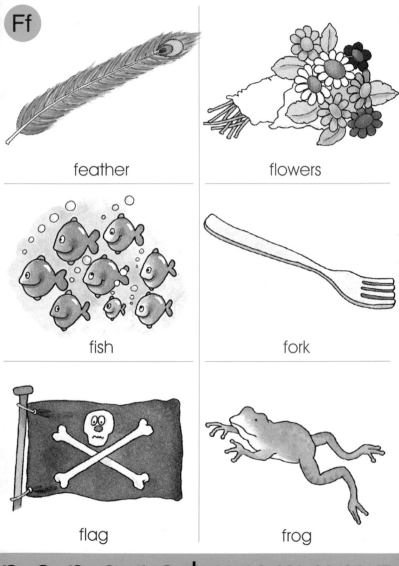

Ff

feather

flowers

fish

fork

flag

frog

Gg

garage

glass

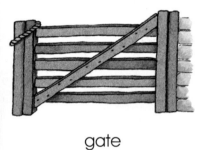

gate

goat

ghost

guitar

Hh

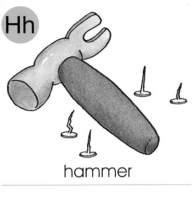

hammer

helicopter

hands

horse

hat

house

Ii

ice cream

instruments

ink

iron

insect

island

Jj

jacket

jug

jam

juggler

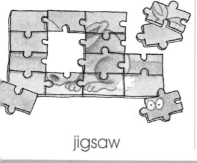

jigsaw

jungle

Kk

kangaroo

knife

keys

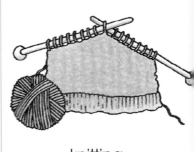

knitting

king

koala

Ll

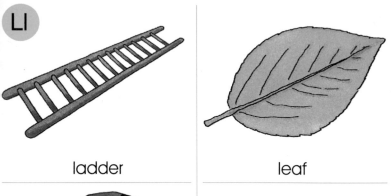

ladder

leaf

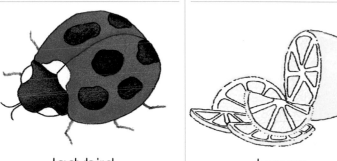

ladybird

lemon

lamp

lion

Mm

map

moon

mirror

mountain

monkey

mouse

Nn

necklace

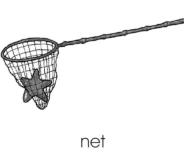

net

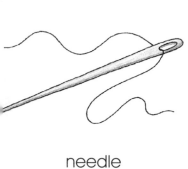

needle

nurse

nest

nuts

Oo

octopus

ostrich

oil

oven

orange

owl

Pp

paint

penguin

palace

piano

pencil

pie

Qq

queen

what's your name?

question

quilt

Rr

rabbit

radio

rainbow

robot

Ss

sheep

rose

shoes

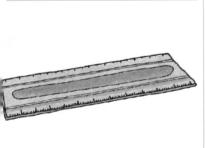

ruler

snake

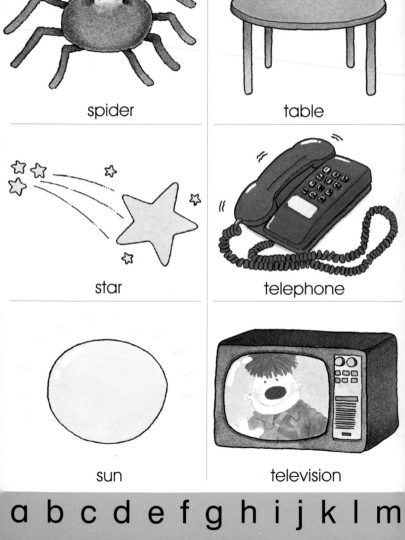

Tt

spider

table

star

telephone

sun

television

tiger

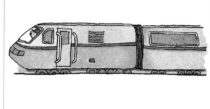

train

tools

tree

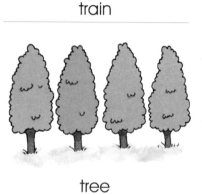

tractor

trumpet

Uu

umbrella

unicorn

uniform

Vv

vegetables

violin

volcano

Ww

watch

whale

waterfall

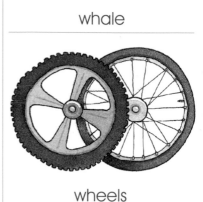

wheels

web

wheelbarrow

whistle

woman

Xx

windmill

X-ray

wolf

xylophone

Yy

yogurt

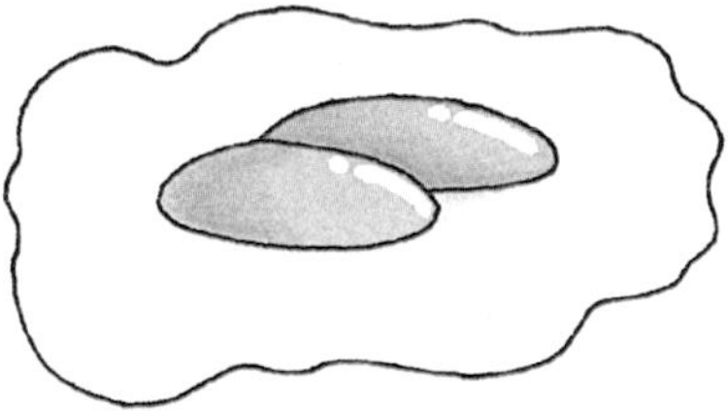

yolk

yo-yo

Zz

zebra

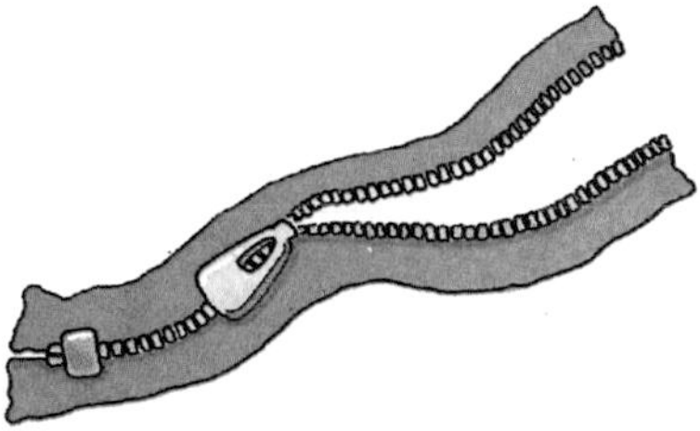

zip

zoo

acrobat
aeroplane
alligator
anchor
apple
astronaut

ball
banana
basket
bird
butterfly

buttons

car
castle
cat
chair
clock
clown

digger
dinosaur
dog
doll
drum
duck

eagle
earrings
egg
elephant

envelope
explorer

feather
fish
flag
flowers
fork
frog

garage
gate
ghost
glass
goat
guitar

hammer
hands
hat
helicopter
horse
house

ice cream
ink
insect
instruments
iron
island

jacket
jam
jigsaw
jug
juggler
jungle

kangaroo
keys
king
knife
knitting
koala

ladder
ladybird
lamp
leaf
lemon
lion